Stuck in this City with You

GEORGIA MITSI

STUCK IN THIS CITY WITH YOU

Published by Lee's Press and Publishing Company
www.LeesPress.net

A Premiere Self-Publishing
Services Company

ISBN-13: *Paperback*
979-8-9860989-6-8

TABLE OF CONTENTS

DEDICATION

To my precious daughter, Eva.

Love,
Mom

ACKNOWLEDGEMENTS

A big thanks to my talented school friend, Lefteris Papathanasis, for the illustration design of me and my daughter for the cover.

INTRODUCTION

"How my daughter is helping me rediscover my identity and 5 more stories of family fun while being in a mandatory lockdown."

Have you ever thought about what it takes to raise bilingual or even better trilingual kids? Kids who grow up in families, where parents are from different countries, have the opportunity to be exposed in richer environments and to speak fluently more than one language. But richer doesn't necessarily mean better. It can be confusing and challenging from time to time. From the parent's point of view, it is amazing being able to give your child the ability to talk in a different language without any extra effort. After all, you have the chance to speak to your mother's tongue every day! However, besides the obvious gift to make your child able to speak in two or sometimes three languages, it is also a huge obligation to transfer all the cultural components of the other country.

This effort involves a lot more than language skills. It is more like trying to constantly balance between two worlds. Living and breathing in one country while trying to keep alive the "other" one; honoring both countries and trying not to make comparisons. Understanding and accepting the fact that your kids' preferences maybe not be the same as yours.

Our childhood memories create a safe place; a warm and peaceful place that we decide to escape when everyday life becomes complicated. It is difficult to realize that your childhood memories may not have lots in common with your children's. Even if you try hard recreating the scenes of your past every summer with them. Their childhood memories will never resemble yours and growing up in a different country is only part of the reason. Time creates erosion. A chasm between reality and imagination.

Being constantly divided between two countries and making silent and sometimes not so silent comparisons do not help either. You must follow the flow of life. You have to let go. Otherwise, you will be stuck in a constant state of unhappiness. It does not matter if your accent is the first thing people comment on. You are not your accent. Instead of treating this as a disadvantage, you can masterfully change it into a nice icebreaker and smile. Being able to create a new life and sometimes a new identity in a foreign environment is proof of your strength. Your accent is a symbol of strength!

It is wonderful to keep alive the communication channel with the family from another country and it's ok if your child does not develop the love for things

4

that you have hoped for. It's great that you continue making your mom's recipes, teaching them songs that you love and watching old movies. But do not get disappointed if they do not share the same love as you for the other country. You may be asking too much! You are asking her to fall in love with an idea, after all. Children, like the rest of us, tend to love what they can touch, hear, see, and smell.

Like her, you also have the right not to adore the same things she does. The difference in preferences may simply indicate the differences in personalities. Carrying the other's country's "baggage" may not be the answer for all the things you don't like. If you treat yourself as an outsider, you will most likely become one. Instead, while keeping your individuality, do try to fit in, keep an open mind and a low guard when dealing with unknown situations. Living in a foreign country is all about becoming comfortable with the unknown. Being comfortable with the uncomfortable. In a way, your ability to grow as a person lies heavily in your ability to navigate through the unknown with a sense of humor. Yes, from time to time, you may have trouble finding the right word or people will ask you to repeat what you said, and you will ask them to do the same. So what? Shake it off and move on!

While you are trying to teach your daughter to speak your language, she will return the favor by correcting your accent and teaching you "cool", new expressions.

She will also show you how to become a better, stronger person because she will give you the motivations you need to keep trying. You will do it because you promised to lead by example. A child needs a parent who keeps the promises, not a perfect parent.

It's important for her to have a family that fits in the current picture. You will continue improving and trying to fit in. Your attitude in life, in combination with her ability to speak in multiple languages will give her a great foundation for life. And who knows? Maybe one day, she may have to live in a foreign country, and only then will she understand the challenge of rediscovering identity.

Chapter 1

SCHOOL

The hardest thing for a parent, when it comes to his kid's education, is to not know what to expect. And I simply do not know. I have no idea how hard SATs are. I don't know how the whole concept of college application works. I had no idea that there is a difference in cut-off age and academic curriculum from state to state! I am still confused about how many pre-Ks exist and what the difference is between pre-K3 and kindergarten.

I am very well educated but the main part of my education took place in a foreign country that uses a totally different educational system. Feelings of inadequacy are hitting me hard because I am not sure if I am pushing my daughter hard enough or too much. I do not share the same craziness about sports as the rest of US parents, but I need to jump on the wagon as she skims through elementary school, middle and high school. I do not attend PTO meetings because I feel that if I express everything I have in my mind, I may develop more enemies than I can handle. I feel

7

that there is too much discussion about the fundraising opportunities but no real discussion about "the elephant in the room", the education part. According to Pearson, the United States ranks fourteenth out of forty countries ranked in that category in 2014.

I come from a culture where people are speaking their minds. Sometimes in ways that may not seem politically correct, but they are not afraid to address the real problem. Here, I am constantly trying to be considerate of others and have learned to communicate their way. It almost feels like walking constantly on ice! But there are certain things that I refuse to change because these are essential parts of who I am. Therefore, sometimes I decide to step back because I feel there is no point in trying to break through all the walls.

I have learned to live and accept certain situations, but I feel totally out of place when I am attending school recitals. Most of the time I am alone, and I envy other couples that show up together. For them it's their community! They may even act in certain ways as a result of some positive peer pressure. My husband and I are not part of the community yet. We are still at the floating stage, like the seed on the flower in Dr. Seuss' book. Floating around, trying to find a place that speaks to our hearts so that we can allow our roots to grow. The marital bond disappeared during the floating process.

My heart just melts every time I see grandparents in

the crowd. My daughter's grandparents will never be able to see her sing or dance. The lights are off and my dark-haired child sings happily lyrics that I cannot even hum and then tears start dripping down on my cheeks and I wish the lights would stay off for a couple more minutes till I regain my coolness.

I hate the fact that I didn't know the local kindergarten songs, the stories, and the games. All these small things are not separate things; they are links to a chain. They carry an untold story of every country's history; they are part of what a culture is made of. It's not the lyrics that I do not know. It's more about the absence of feelings. These stories, the songs, and the games, do not speak to my heart because I have no memories associated with them. Feelings of emptiness and disconnect with my own blood that I cannot ignore.

Chapter 2

THE BIRTHDAY PARTY

The "cookie-cutter" approach is something I detest. It requires less energy and saves you from headaches, but it strips out any individuality, creativity, and excitement. It can be found across America from buildings to business proposals, to dressing styles to birthday parties.

Oh! The Birthday party phenomenon that I am trying to understand for the past 18 years and play it by the rules. The one that starts with an Evite invitation sent well in advance, meaning a month or more ahead. The one that I dread not to forget is to RSVP.

The one that involves 90 minutes of "fun" that comes with a specific price tag and a structured agenda: 5-10 minutes of expected arrival time, 50 minutes of play, 25 minutes of eating pizza and cutting the cake, 5-10 minutes of pick-up procedures. The same agenda. Repeatedly. Pizza, cupcakes, or cake, some kind of activity and boom! Out of the room. Another year went by, celebrated in style… Thank you notes must be prepared and sent within a week.

As a mom, I am not satisfied. I don't think that I

am putting any extra effort to make my child feel extra special. Paying hundreds of dollars does not translate in her mind as being loved because this is what we do on a regular basis. Certainly, it does not translate in my mind as doing something extraordinaire to celebrate another year of love, smiles, and changes.

I want to "open" my house and my heart and welcome her friends inside our world that may be a bit different from theirs. I want to get to know the special people in her life. I want to treat them like we do in my home country. After all, Greece is known for its hospitality and warmth. I want to show them that during her special day, our home is their home; that they are part of our family. Open a door to her life and allow them to get to know her better. I want to cook and bake for them. It does not matter that I am not a great cook. It's my way for showing my appreciation to them for being good friends to my child. It's my way for recognizing the importance of creating childhood memories together. I want them to be silly and use their creativity and imagination. I want to give them the time to relax and enjoy. To just sit and giggle around!

What's the point of having a celebration if strict agendas strip out any celebratory vibe?

I am wondering how these kids might feel since all parties follow such a repetitive schedule. Are they actually looking forward to participating in parties that do not promise any excitement? Is modern parenting too handholding? Allowing kids to deal with unknown "territories", it gives them the chance to become flexible and adaptable. Both important skills in the grown-up world.

Should we, as parents, follow the monotonous "recipe" or dare to disrupt the common theme with a celebration that lasts 3 hours, have just a basic schedule and allow kids to interact and find ways to spend creatively time together? I am afraid that if we keep holding their hands tight, even during events that supposed to be fun and easy, they will develop a serious problem adapting to situations where social interaction in unknown situations is required. In real life situations without agendas, they will stay in the corner and keep their heads buried down on their shoulders while they will pretend reading something super "important" on their portable screens. I think, especially now, we have a huge responsibility as parents to pay extra attention and try honing as much as possible our children's social skills.

Let's disrupt the birthdays and transform them to something less boring than a corporate meeting!

Chapter 3

THE HOMEWORK

To my experience so far, in US, playdates are complicated. Unnecessarily complicated!

It seems that there is a play-date etiquette that a parent needs to learn in order not to screw up her children's social life. Etiquette created by well-educated, obsessed-to-detail mothers and pushed upon the rest of us. An etiquette that has transformed a simple playdate to a Board of Directors meeting that comes with an invite, agenda, diet considerations and scheduling conflicts. But most importantly with a strict ending time.

When real meetings are happening consequently, with real agendas about the job that brings food to our table, I simply refuse to play by the rules. I tried it! But it created so much extra pressure on me that I decided to be more selective even if that led eventually to burning certain bridges.

Receiving specific instructions on the foods that I was allowed to offer (besides allergies), it almost felt insulting! My stressing out by being 10 minutes late because of traffic and finding my child waiting on the door, made me and my child feel unwelcome. Answering to at least of couple of emails during my daughter's 2-hour playdate, it felt exhausting. Responding to a nasty email criticizing my parenting skills because I allowed the kids to have access to an iPad and listen to a song that sounded inappropriate (even if it was played later at the school's celebration), it's a time not well spent.

The playdates I remember used to be special and fun. There was a sense of trust between moms. They knew that their kids would be well taken care of. They knew that the playdate was meant to create an opportunity for the other mom to get some down time. Not to create extra work and not to add extra stress. Moms back then used to share a secret code of camaraderie. Moms will always compare and criticize but they should also be supportive and understanding of each other.

Today, moms are under lots of pressure. Internal and external pressures have created the modern-mom stereotype that treats parenting more like a regular job. It's a hell of a job! But not in the traditional way. No job description can adequately encapsulate the duties related to being a mom. There is no project that can be more rewarding than being a mom. There is no job offer that brings such a joy and sense of fulfillment than being a mom.

Moms do not work. Moms create, sustain, and develop lives. Moms are being asked to innovate and disrupt every day because this is the only way to keep up with young, evolving minds. Moms are being asked to lead by love and understanding and offer always superior "customer service". Moms easily can keep the competition at bay because each mom has a unique set of offerings tailored specifically to her offspring's' needs.

Therefore, moms, let's enjoy the beautiful gift of parenting with less pressure because we are all special in our own unique way!

Chapter 4

DOCTOR'S APPOINTMENT

For those of you that have never thought about it, imagine saying or hearing "I love you" in a language different from your native language. Does it sound the same? Does it manage to "produce" butterflies in your stomach? Similarly, when you are in pain, maybe hearing words of encouragement in your native language can make you feel better?

I have never imagined that during what it seemed like a never-ending delivery (twenty hours), I would have to communicate in English and Spanish. I consider myself lucky because I speak English quite fluently and I could understand some Spanish. But when the contractions began and the pain "paralyzed" my mind, I felt so strong the need to communicate in my mother tongue. Eighteen years later, the voices of the nurses, still echo in my head with a mixed sound of "push" and "empuje".

Needless to say, that when bad things happen - no one can escape them - and I find myself escorting my child to the ER, it is when the pressure hits me the hardest. This is the time where there is no time for grammatical errors. There is no time for trying to dig up the right word from my mind. There is no time for inadequacies!

But it is exactly in those moments where you wish with every cell of your existence to have someone to talk to in your mother tongue. Of course, miracles can happen and from time to time you can bump into a doctor that speaks into your heart and the non-verbal cues can ease your worries.

Most of the time, you are being stuck in a situation; you are scared (ready to pee in your pants type of scared) but you are trying to be calm and present the case as accurately as possible and then try to understand the rules and the hospital etiquette, as much as you can. Then you have to memorize the Fahrenheit, the inches, the pounds and the name of all the drugs used. But guess what? You cannot because for thirty years your brain has been trained to memorize in Celsius, centimeters, and kilos. And you feel, not exactly stupid but not quite yourself. You leave the hospital in a hurry; holding your child's hand firmly in one hand and on the other one, you hold the printed version of the instructions given. You hold onto that piece of paper like the golden ticket in Willy Wonka's movie because you know that by the time you arrive home you will remember only 70% or less of what the doctor told you.

You drive home knowing that your child will recover. You let the pressure go and as it goes, silent tears start coming down your face and you swear inside your head in a chimera of curses by leveraging all the best that each language, you have learned so far, has to offer.

Chapter 5

DECISIONS

There are days when senses are more sensitive. The light becomes weaker, the temperatures are dropping, life settles into a monotonous pace and the summer photos can no longer "warm" your heart. Warm nostalgia combined with a strong sense of mortality "pushes" you to re-evaluate the situation. Once again!

And after dinner, secretly you share the common secret with your spouse.

- I cannot envision myself getting older in this foreign place.

You take it one step further and with pompous voice, you add:

- I don't want to leave my bones here!

Silence.

You have made this discussion in the past. Too many times! You both carefully avoid addressing the dying question. But other than that, you both know that the window of opportunity has closed for you. There is no turning back!

You have to face the facts. The period of denial is over. And like with every loss you have to allow yourself time to mourn and heal. You will never be able to forget the memories. You will always wonder how different things could have been if... But like with every loss, you cannot revive the past and live with the memories forever. You have to learn how to let go!

Your hearts will always be there, but your minds are here. This is a hard reality to face but the only reality you really have.

Your children's hearts and minds are here.

They recognize as their home, the yellow house that sits in a nestled by trees neighborhood. For them, going back home means returning to the yellow house. For you, going back home is returning to your roots, where childhood memories live among the belongings you never had the chance to bring over. Their childhood memories are part of this house, the one you treat as a temporary place.

As parents we know how important it is for kids to have a routine, a base and not to disrupt it. Do I have the right as a parent to act selfishly? Can I take my family and move back to where I feel more comfortable even if I make them uncomfortable? Can a happier parent help a child adjust easier to a new environment? What if the move does not end up being a good decision? As a parent to what extent can I experiment?

These questions and a lot more put bumps in the road of our monotone life and "spice" things up. They are part of the "simple talk" in our household.

Chapter 6

STUCK IN THE CITY… WITH YOU!

When I decided to share my experiences and the challenges of the modern world as a 1st generation immigrant, I thought the main point of the effort was to emphasize my feelings of being stuck in the middle. I have been living away from my parents' home for more than half of my life. Keeping in mind that I have no memories associated with the first years of my existence, the years away are even more.

However, as I am contemplating about my life's events, I realize that I am far from being stuck in the middle. Maybe my agonizing effort to deal with the facts led me to my catharsis. I no longer feel that I am stuck in the middle!

I feel that life caught me by surprise on many occasions. I was not fully prepared and lots of times I handled things far from graciously. I suffered from a serious case of nostalgia up to a point that I was mostly re-living in the past. I was stuck in the past and

I became frustrated and lonely because the world seemed so unfair. I made mistakes! I lost good people from my life because I was too scared to open up and bring them closer to me. I lost opportunities because I couldn't make long-term plans. I lost parts of myself because I had to survive in a world that was not my choice.

I realize now that I cannot continue beating myself up for all the mistakes. I paid the price and accepted the consequences of my actions. I am learning to be kinder with others and myself. I am learning to not take others and myself too seriously. I never thought that in my forties I would have to work so much on self-improvement and feeling happy while doing it.

Most importantly, after all these years of loneliness, I finally realized that I am not alone. There are lots of people out there who feel the same. I may not know them personally, but they exist out there, share the same feelings and deal with the same challenges.

For all these people that I will never meet but we have so much in common, I hope this confession gives them some peace and some much-needed connection. We are not alone!

Besides my initial goal to find some peace through the catharsis of putting my thoughts and emotions into writing, I also created this confession as an attempt to develop a stronger bond with my daughter who has seen me at my best and my worst. A special gift to my daughter who just turned 18!

To tell her how guilty I feel and how sorry I am. Although I tried every day to make a conscious effort to be a good mom who listens and cares for her, I am not always satisfied with my performance. I have lost years of her life because I made my job the main priority. I have lost years of her life because I was too stressed with my job. I allowed joyous moments to disappear in front of my eyes because I was stuck in everything I have left behind. I ruined family vacations and Christmas celebrations because part of my self was absent, mourning for being so far away from home. I was unable to enjoy my life here because I was stuck in a life far, far away from here!

I cannot turn back the clock. What I can do though is to cherish my everyday life here in my adopted country, share some good laughs and do silly things with my precious daughter. Because there are lots of people out there who don't even have the chance to re-build a life in a second country. There are lots of people out there who wished to have a precious child. There are lots of people out there who wished to have more time to do silly things with their children and they simply can't.

Her well-being is my number one priority! I realized through trial and error, lots of reading and soul-searching, what a child needs the most is to be loved by real, human parents! Parents who are not authoritative figures and are not scared of showing their faults and weaknesses. Children need to be loved by real people who are not afraid to say, "I don't know, let's Google it together". People who can easily admit their mistakes and move on. People who find solutions to problems and do not quit the fight. People who admit that life is not easy but with clear mind, hard work and optimism, challenges can be handled. People who say that few times you win but most of the times you will learn.

Being a 1st generation immigrant turned out to being actually a blessing! There are so many things that I don't know and haven't seen so I am in a constant mode of learning and discovering. From words to roads, to traditions, to songs to culture. Subtle reminders of my humble presence. I couldn't easily hide my inefficiencies and pretend. I needed to make a conscious effort and fight my way through it. For years, I was unsatisfied with my personal progress because I had envisioned myself so differently as a person and as a parent. A parent who knows everything. A parent who never makes mistakes, a parent who is above and beyond. After a while, I realized that this was simply not possible under the current circumstances. I don't think it's possible under any circumstances, but it took me 18 years to realize! I accepted myself which is far from being perfect and I finally felt free and closer to my child.

25

I grew up in an environment where I thought for many years that my parents knew everything, and I blindly trusted their judgment. Many bad things occurred because of that. The moment I decided to accept the flawed relationship I had with my parents; the bad experiences lost their powerful influence in my life's outcome.

I know now that it's important for my daughter to know that I am far from perfect. I want her to be confident and trust her gut feelings. I want her to challenge me because it pushes me to continuously work on my self-improvement. I believe that if she sees in me a person who is constantly trying for self-improvement, it will be a far more valuable life-lesson. This will allow us to develop a deep and true relationship where we figure out life together, and to contribute discovering life's mysteries with the unique view that each one of us has. She will bring her spontaneity, energy, freshness and stubbornness and I will bring calmness, experience, and flexibility to the extent possible.

Life is a beautiful journey and I want her to be my backpack mate till our roads separate!

Chapter 7

STUCK IN THE CITY WITH YOU... DURING COVID!

And then COVID came, and all my previous challenges intensified. I found myself literally STUCK in this city with you! Actually, I was stuck with you...even worse... in the comfort of our house! For months...many months....

And suddenly all my previous problems felt so much more manageable.

Stuck in the house with a teenage daughter while we were both going through the pain of the divorce.

It literally sucks...

My feelings of loneliness hit like a tsunami. A never-ending one...I felt like holding onto the mast of my small craft being hit by huge waves in an open sea and holding on for dear life, simply because I had no other choice. As the number of cases grew exponentially and the whole world paralyzed, the storm continued, and my spirit almost gave up. I only wish I could take a plane and go to see my parents! There were many times that I just needed a hug.

It is worth fighting when there are options. What options did I have, other than waiting?

In this new world of fear there weren't any. Nobody knows when things will go back to normal. Besides wearing a mask and washing your hands there are not a lot of other ways to contribute. At least in a war, you know that you can fight for your survival. You can contribute somehow to the battle. In the COVID dominated world, I felt helpless, but I couldn't just sit back and wait. I had to continue working online which practically meant non-stop. I had to continue dealing with my kids' disappointment and despair of missing their normal childhood.

How can you keep trying when no options are available?

They say that you cannot fight or worry about things that are out of your control. Accept the fate! Accept the COVID dominated world! Maybe this is World War 3...because we knew that this "war" would be different.

People died, economies collapsed, there was so much trauma and despair. The emotional and financial wounds of this pandemic will take years to heal.

Remember my little troubles of the school, the parent-related pressure, the birthdays, the doctor's appointments? Guess what? Nothing looks the same anymore. There is no school, no playmates, no parent pressure, no birthdays, no doctors' appointments. In my case, there was not even a husband ...someone to lean on.

It was just my kids and I living alone in our virtual bubble, trying to communicate with the world via a screen. I am not complaining. We survived this.

Through gratitude. Because it was my only defense. We are still together. We have a roof over our heads and lots of food to eat. We have our love for each other.

I better hold onto that mast of my beaten up, little craft for as long as my heart beats. Because this is what moms do. They never give up no matter how ruff the waters get. And I do not wish for a different life or calmer waters. Not anymore. This is my beautiful, courageous journey, I hold on to the mast with all my regained strength because my journey has a purpose. I need to bring my girl safe to the shore. To the shore of the new world.